MOLIÈRE

THE MISANTHROPE

Comedy In Five Acts, 1666

Translated into English Verse by
RICHARD WILBUR

DRAMATISTS PLAY SERVICE INC.

To Harry Levin

INTRODUCTION

The idea that comedy is a ritual in which society's laughter corrects individual extravagance is particularly inapplicable to *The Misanthrope*. In this play, society itself is indicted, and though Alceste's criticisms are indiscriminate, they are not unjustified. It is true that falseness and intrigue are everywhere on view; the conventions enforce a routine dishonesty, justice is subverted by influence, love is overwhelmed by calculation, and these things are accepted, even by the best, as "natural." The cold vanity of Oronte, Acaste, and Clitandre, the malignant hypocrisy of Arsinoé, the insincerity of Célimène, are to be taken as exemplary of the age, and Philinte's philosophic tolerance will not quite do in response to such a condition of things. The honest Eliante is the one we are most to trust, and this is partly because she sees that Alceste's intransigence *A quelque chose en soy de noble & d'héroïque*.

But *The Misanthrope* is not only a critique of society; it is also a study of impurity of motive in a critic of society. If Alceste has a rage for the genuine, and he truly has, it is unfortunately compromised and exploited by his vast, unconscious egotism. He is a jealous friend *(Je veux qu'on me distingue)*, and it is Philinte's polite effusiveness toward another which prompts his attack on promiscuous civility. He is a jealous lover, and his "frankness" about Oronte's sonnet owes something to the fact that Oronte is his rival, and that the sonnet is addressed to Célimène. Like many humorless and indignant people, he is hard on everybody but himself, and does not perceive it when he fails his own ideal. In one aspect, Alceste seems a moral giant misplaced in a trivial society, having (in George Eliot's phrase) "a certain spiritual grandeur ill-matched with the

5

meanness of opportunity"; in another aspect, he seems an unconscious fraud who magnifies the petty faults of others in order to dramatize himself in his own eyes.

He is, of course, both at once: but the two impressions predominate by turns. A victim, like all around him, of the moral enervation of the times, he cannot consistently be the Man of Honor—simple, magnanimous, passionate, decisive, true. It is his distinction that he is aware of that ideal, and that he can fitfully embody it; his comic flaw consists in a Quixotic confusion of himself with the ideal, a willingness to distort the world for his own self-deceptive and histrionic purposes. Paradoxically, then, the advocate of true feeling and honest intercourse is the one character most artificial, most out-of-touch, most in danger of that nonentity and solitude which all, in the chattery, hollow world of this play, are fleeing. He must play-act continually in order to believe in his own existence, and he welcomes the fact or show of injustice as a dramatic cue. At the close of the play, when Alceste has refused to appeal his lawsuit and has spurned the hand of Célimène, one cannot escape the suspicion that his indignation is in great part instrumental, a desperate means of counterfeiting an identity.

Martin Turnell (whose book *The Classical Moment* contains a fine analysis of *The Misanthrope*) observes that those speeches of Alceste which ring most false are, as it were, parodies of "Cornelian *tirade.*" To duplicate this parody-tragic effect in English it was clearly necessary to keep the play in verse, where it would be possible to control the tone more sharply, and to recall our own tragic tradition. There were other reasons, too, for approximating Molière's form. The constant of rhythm and rhyme was needed, in the translation as in the original, for bridging great gaps between high comedy and farce, lofty diction and ordinary talk, deep character and shallow. Again, while prose might preserve the thematic structure of the play, other "musical" elements would be lost, in particular the frequently intricate arrangements of balancing half-lines, lines, couplets, quatrains, and sestets. There is no question that words, when dancing within such patterns, are not their prosaic selves, but have a wholly different mood and meaning.

Consider, finally, two peculiarities of the dialogue of the play: redundancy and logic. When Molière has a character repeat essentially the same thing in three successive couplets, it will sometimes have a very clear dramatic point; but it will always have the intention of stabilizing the idea against the movement of the verse, and of giving a specifically rhetorical pleasure. In a prose rendering, these latter effects are lost, and the passage tends to seem merely prolix. As for logic, it is a convention of *The Misanthrope* that its main characters can express themselves logically, and in the most complex grammar; Molière's dramatic verse, which is almost wholly free of metaphor, derives much of its richness from argumentative virtuosity. Here is a bit of logic from Arsinoé:

Madame, l'Amitié doit sur tout éclater
Aux choses qui le plus nous peuvent importer:
Et comme il n'en est point de plus grande importance
Que celles de l'Honneur et de la Bienséance,
Je viens par un avis qui touche vostre honneur
Témoigner l'amitié que pour vous a mon Coeur.

In prose it might come out like this: "Madam, friendship should most display itself when truly vital matters are in question: and since there are no things more vital than decency and honor, I have come to prove my heartfelt friendship by giving you some advice which concerns your reputation." Even if that were better rendered, it would still be plain that Molière's logic loses all its baroque exuberance in prose; it sounds lawyerish; without rhyme and verse to phrase and emphasize the steps of its progression, the logic becomes obscure like Congreve's, not crystalline and followable as it was meant to be.

For all these reasons, rhymed verse seemed to me obligatory. The choice did not preclude accuracy, and what follows is, I believe, a line-for-line verse translation quite as faithful as any which have been done in prose. I hasten to say that I am boasting only of patience; a translation may, alas, be faithful on all counts, and still lack quality.

One word about diction. This is a play in which French aristocrats of 1666 converse about their special concerns, and employ the moral and philosophical terms peculiar to their thought. Not all my words, therefore, are strictly modern; I had for example to use "spleen" and "phlegm"; but I think that I have avoided the zounds sort of thing, and that at best the diction mediates between then and now, suggesting no one period. There are occasional vulgarities, but for these there is precedent in the original, Moliere's people being aristocrats and therefore not genteel.

If this English version is played or read aloud, the names should be pronounced in a fashion *roughly* French, without nasal and uvular agonies. Damon should be *dah-MOAN*, and for rhythmic convenience Arsinoé should be *ar-SIN-oh-eh*.

My translation was begun in late 1952 in New Mexico, during a fellowship from the Guggenheim Foundation, and finished this year in Rome under grants from the American Academy of Arts & Letters and the Chapelbrook Foundation. To these organizations, and to certain individuals who have befriended the project, I am very grateful.

R.W.

Wellesley, Massachusetts.

CHARACTERS

ALCESTE . . . . in love with Célimène
PHILINTE . . . . Alceste's friend
ORONTE . . . . in love with Célimène
CELIMENE . . . . Alceste's beloved
ELIANTE . . . . Célimène's cousin
ARSINOE . . . . a friend of Célimène's
ACASTE . . . . marquess
CLITANDRE . . . . marquess
BASQUE . . . . Célimène's servant
A GUARD . . . . of the Marshalsea
DUBOIS . . . . Alceste's valet

The scene throughout is in Célimène's house at Paris.

First produced by The Poet's Theatre, Cambridge, on October 25th, 1955.

9

THE MISANTHROPE

ACT I
SCENE ONE

PHILANTE, ALCESTE

PHILINTE.
Now, what's got into you?
ALCESTE. *(Seated.)*

         Kindly leave me alone.

PHILINTE.
Come, come, what is it? This lugubrious tone...
ALCESTE.
Leave me, I said; you spoil my solitude.
PHILINTE.
Oh, listen to me, now, and don't be rude.
ALCESTE.
I choose to be rude, Sir, and to be hard of hearing.
PHILINTE.
These ugly moods of yours are not endearing;
Friends though we are, I really must insist...
ALCESTE. *(Abruptly rising.)*
Friends? Friends, you say? Well, cross me off your list.
I've been your friend till now, as you well know;
But after what I saw a moment ago
I tell you flatly that our ways must part.
I wish no place in a dishonest heart.
PHILINTE.
Why, what have I done, Alceste? Is this quite just?
ALCESTE.
My God, you ought to die of self-disgust.
I call your conduct inexcusable, Sir,
And every man of honor will concur.

I see you almost hug a man to death,
Exclaim for joy until you're out of breath,
And supplement these loving demonstrations
With endless offers, vows, and protestations;
Then when I ask you "Who was that?", I find
that you can barely bring his name to mind!
Once the man's back is turned, you cease to love him,
And speak with absolute indifference of him!
By God, I say it's base and scandalous
To falsify the heart's affections thus;
If I caught myself behaving in such a way,
I'd hang myself for shame, without delay.
PHILINTE.
It hardly seems a hanging matter to me;
I hope that you will take it graciously
If I extend myself a slight reprieve,
And live a little longer, by your leave.
ALCESTE.
How dare you joke about a crime so grave?
PHILINTE.
What crime? How else are people to behave?
ALCESTE.
I'd have them be sincere, and never part
With any word that isn't from the heart.
PHILINTE.
When someone greets us with a show of pleasure,
It's but polite to give him equal measure,
Return his love the best that we know how,
And trade him offer for offer, vow for vow.
ALCESTE.
No, no, this formula you'd have me follow,
However fashionable, is false and hollow,
And I despise the frenzied operations
Of all these barterers of protestations,
These lavishers of meaningless embraces,
These utterers of obliging commonplaces,

Who court and flatter everyone on earth
And praise the fool no less than the man of worth.
Should you rejoice that someone fondles you,
Offers his love and service, swears to be true,
And fills your ears with praises of your name,
When to the first damned fop he'll say the same?
No, no: no self-respecting heart would dream
Of prizing so promiscuous an esteem;
However high the praise, there's nothing worse
Than sharing honors with the universe.
Esteem is founded on comparison:
To honor all men is to honor none.
Since you embrace this indiscriminate vice,
Your friendship comes at far too cheap a price;
I spurn the easy tribute of a heart
Which will not set the worthy man apart:
I choose, Sir, to be chosen; and in fine,
The friend of mankind is no friend of mine.
PHILINTE.
But in polite society, custom decrees
That we show certain outward courtesies...
ALCESTE.
Ah, no! we should condemn with all our force
Such false and artificial intercourse.
Let men behave like men; let them display
Their inmost hearts in everything they say;
Let the heart speak, and let our sentiments
Not mask themselves in silly compliments.
PHILINTE.
In certain cases it would be uncouth
And most absurd to speak the naked truth;
With all respect for your exalted notions,
It's often best to veil one's true emotions.
Wouldn't the social fabric come undone
If we were wholly frank with everyone?
Suppose you met with someone you couldn't bear;
Would you inform him of it then and there?

ALCESTE.
Yes.
PHILINTE.

Then you'd tell old Emilie it's pathetic
The way she daubs her features with cosmetic
And plays the gay coquette at sixty-four?
ALCESTE.
I would.
PHILINTE.

And you'd call Dorilas a bore,
And tell him every ear at court is lame
From hearing him brag about his noble name?
ALCESTE.
Precisely.
PHILINTE.

Ah, you're joking.
ALCESTE.

Au contraire:
In this regard there's none I'd choose to spare.
All are corrupt; there's nothing to be seen
In court or town but aggravates my spleen.
I fall into deep gloom and melancholy
When I survey the scene of human folly,
Finding on every hand base flattery,
Injustice, fraud, self-interest, treachery....
Ah, it's too much; mankind has grown so base,
I mean to break with the whole human race.
PHILINTE.

This philosophic rage is a bit extreme;
You've no idea how comical you seem;
Indeed, we're like those brothers in the play
Called *School for Husbands,* one of whom was prey...
ALCESTE.

Enough, now! None of your stupid similes.
PHILINTE.

Then let's have no more tirades, if you please.

The world won't change, whatever you say or do;
And since plain speaking means so much to you,
I'll tell you plainly that by being frank
You've earned the reputation of a crank,
And that you're thought ridiculous when you rage
And rant against the manners of the age.
ALCESTE.
So much the better; just what I wish to hear.
No news could be more grateful to my ear.
All men are so detestable in my eyes,
I should be sorry if they thought me wise.
PHILINTE.
Your hatred's very sweeping, is it not?
ALCESTE.
Quite right: I hate the whole degraded lot.
PHILINTE.
Must all poor human creatures be embraced,
Without distinction, by your vast distaste?
Even in these bad times, there are surely a few...
ALCESTE.
No, I include all men in one dim view:
Some men I hate for being rogues; the others
I hate because they treat the rogues like brothers,
And, lacking a virtuous scorn for what is vile,
Receive the villain with a complaisant smile.
Notice how tolerant people choose to be
Toward that bold rascal who's at law with me.
His social polish can't conceal his nature;
One sees at once that he's a treacherous creature;
No one could possibly be taken in
By those soft speeches and that sugary grin.
The whole world knows the shady means by which
The low-brow's grown so powerful and rich,
And risen to a rank so bright and high
That virtue can but blush, and merit sigh.
Whenever his name comes up in conversation,

None will defend his wretched reputation;
Call him knave, liar, scoundrel, and all the rest,
Each head will nod, and no one will protest.
And yet his smirk is seen in every house,
He's greeted everywhere with smiles and bows,
And when there's any honor that can be got
By pulling strings, he'll get it, like as not.
My God! It chills my heart to see the ways
Men come to terms with evil nowadays;
Sometimes, I swear, I'm moved to flee and find
Some desert land unfouled by humankind.

PHILINTE.
Come, let's forget the follies of the times
And pardon mankind for its petty crimes;
Let's have an end of rantings and of railings,
And show some leniency toward human failings.
This world requires a pliant rectitude;
Too stern a virtue makes one stiff and rude;
Good sense views all extremes with detestation,
And bids us to be noble in moderation.
The rigid virtues of the ancient days
Are not for us; they jar with all our ways
And ask of us too lofty a perfection.
Wise men accept their times without objection,
And there's no greater folly, if you ask me,
Than trying to reform society.
Like you, I see each day a hundred and one
Unhandsome deeds that might be better done,
But still, for all the faults that meet my view,
I'm never known to storm and rave like you.
I take men as they are, or let them be,
And teach my soul to bear their frailty;
And whether in court or town, whatever the scene,
My phlegm's as philosophic as your spleen.

ALCESTE.
This phlegm which you so eloquently commend,

Does nothing ever rile it up, my friend?
Suppose some man you trust should treacherously
Conspire to rob you of your property,
And do his best to wreck your reputation?
Wouldn't you feel a certain indignation?
PHILINTE.
Why, no. These faults of which you so complain
Are part of human nature, I maintain,
And it's no more a matter for disgust
That men are knavish, selfish and unjust,
Than that the vulture dines upon the dead,
And wolves are furious, and apes ill-bred.
ALCESTE.
Shall I see myself betrayed, robbed, torn to bits,
And not...Oh, let's be still and rest our wits.
Enough of reasoning, now. I've had my fill.
PHILINTE.
Indeed, you would do well, Sir, to be still.
Rage less at your opponent, and give some thought
To how you'll win this lawsuit that he's brought.
ALCESTE.
I assure you I'll do nothing of the sort.
PHILINTE.
Then who will plead your case before the court?
ALCESTE.
Reason and right and justice will plead for me.
PHILINTE.
Oh, Lord. What judges do you plan to see?
ALCESTE.
Why, none. the justice of my cause is clear.
PHILINTE.
Of course, man; but there's politics to fear...
ALCESTE.
No, I refuse to lift a hand. That's flat.
I'm either right, or wrong.

17

PHILINTE.

Don't count on that.

ALCESTE.
No, I'll do nothing.
PHILINTE.

Your enemy's influence

Is great, you know...
ALCESTE.

That makes no difference.

PHILINTE.
It will; you'll see.
ALCESTE.

Must honor bow to guile?

If so, I shall be proud to lose the trial.
PHILINTE.
Oh, really...
ALCESTE.

I'll discover by this case

Whether or not men are sufficiently base
And impudent and villainous and perverse
To do me wrong before the universe.
PHILINTE.
What a man!
ALCESTE.

Oh, I could wish, whatever the cost,

Just for the beauty of it, that my trial were lost.
PHILINTE.
If people heard you talking so, Alceste,
They'd split their sides. Your name would be a jest.
ALCESTE.
So much the worse for jesters.
PHILINTE.

May I enquire

Whether this rectitude you so admire,
And these hard virtues you're enamored of
Are qualities of the lady whom you love?

18

It much surprises me that you, who seem
To view mankind with furious disesteem,
Have yet found something to enchant your eyes
Amidst a species which you so despise.
And what is more amazing, I'm afraid,
Is the most curious choice your heart has made.
The honest Eliante is fond of you,
Arsinoe, the prude, admires you too;
And yet your spirit's been perversely led
To choose the flighty Célimène instead,
Whose brittle malice and coquettish ways
So typify the manners of our days.
How is it that the traits you most abhor
Are bearable in this lady you adore?
Are you so blind with love that you can't find them?
Or do you contrive, in her case, not to mind them?
ALCESTE.
My love for that young widow's not the kind
That can't perceive defects; no, I'm not blind.
I see her faults, despite my ardent love,
And all I see I fervently reprove.
And yet I'm weak; for all her falsity,
That woman knows the art of pleasing me,
And though I never cease complaining of her,
I swear I cannot manage not to love her.
Her charm outweighs her faults; I can but aim
To cleanse her spirit in my love's pure flame.
PHILINTE.
That's no small task; I wish you all success.
You think then that she loves you?
ALCESTE.

                                          Heavens, yes!
I wouldn't love her did she not love me.
PHILINTE.
Well, if her taste for you is plain to see,
Why do these rivals cause you such despair?

19

ALCESTE.
True love, Sir, is possessive, and cannot bear
To share with all the world. I'm here today
To tell her she must send that mob away.
PHILINTE.
If I were you, and had your choice to make,
Eliante, her cousin, would be the one I'd take;
That honest heart, which cares for you alone,
Would harmonize far better with your own.
ALCESTE.
True, true: each day my reason tells me so;
But reason doesn't rule in love, you know.
PHILINTE.
I fear some bitter sorrow is in store;
This love...

SCENE TWO

ORONTE, ALCESTE, PHILINTE

ORONTE. *(To Alceste.)*
          The servants told me at the door
That Eliante and Célimène were out,
But when I heard, dear Sir, that you were about,
I came to say, without exaggeration,
That I hold you in the vastest admiration,
And that it's always been my dearest desire
To be the friend of one I so admire.
I hope to see my love of merit requited,
And you and me in friendship's bond united.
I'm sure you won't refuse—if I may be frank—
A friend of my devotedness—and rank.
(During this speech of Oronte's, Alceste is abstracted, and seems unaware

*that he is being spoken to. He only breaks off his reverie when
Oronte says:)*
It was for you, if you please, that my words were intended.
ALCESTE.
For me, Sir?
ORONTE.
Yes, for you. You're not offended?
ALCESTE.
By no means. But this much surprises me...
The honor comes most unexpectedly...
ORONTE.
My high regard should not astonish you;
The whole world feels the same. It is your due.
ALCESTE.
Sir...
ORONTE.
Why, in all the State there isn't one
Can match your merits; they shine, Sir, like the sun.
ALCESTE.
Sir...
ORONTE.
You are higher in my estimation
Than all that's most illustrious in the nation.
ALCESTE.
Sir...
ORONTE.
If I lie, may heaven strike me dead!
To show you that I mean what I have said,
Permit me, Sir, to embrace you most sincerely,
And swear that I will prize our friendship dearly.
Give me your hand. And now, Sir, if you choose,
We'll make our vows.
ALCESTE.
Sir...
ORONTE.
What! You refuse?

21

ALCESTE.
Sir, it's a very great honor you extend:
But friendship is a sacred thing, my friend;
It would be profanation to bestow
The name of friend on one you hardly know.
All parts are better played when well-rehearsed;
Let's put off friendship, and get aquainted first.
We may discover it would be unwise
To try to make our natures harmonize.
ORONTE.
By heaven! You're sagacious to the core;
This speech has made me admire you even more.
Let time, then, bring us closer day by day;
Meanwhile, I shall be yours in every way.
If, for example, there should be anything
You wish at court, I'll mention it to the King.
I have his ear, of course; it's quite well known
That I am much in favor with the throne.
In short, I am your servant. And now, dear friend,
Since you have such fine judgement, I intend
To please you, if I can, with a small sonnet
I wrote not long ago. Please comment on it,
And tell me whether I ought to publish it.
ALCESTE.
You must excuse me, Sir; I'm hardly fit
To judge such matters.
ORONTE.
                              Why not?
ALCESTE.
                                                  I am, I fear,
Inclined to be unfashionably sincere.
ORONTE.
Just what I ask; I'd take no satisfaction
In anything but your sincere reaction.
I beg you not to dream of being kind.

ALCESTE.
Since you desire it, Sir, I'll speak my mind.
ORONTE.
Sonnet. It's a sonnet...*Hope*...The poem's addressed
To a lady who wakened hopes within my breast.
Hope...this is not the pompous sort of thing,
Just modest little verses, with a tender ring.
ALCESTE.
Well, we shall see.
ORONTE.

                       Hope... I'm anxious to hear
Whether the style seems properly smooth and clear,
And whether the choice of words is good or bad.
ALCESTE.
We'll see, we'll see.
ORONTE.

                    Perhaps I ought to add
That it took me only a quarter-hour to write it.
ALCESTE.
The time's irrelevant, Sir: kindly recite it.
ORONTE. *(Reading.)*
Hope comforts us awhile, t'is true,
Lulling our cares with careless laughter,
And yet such joy is full of rue,
My Phyllis, if nothing follows after.
PHILINTE.
I'm charmed by this already; the style's delightful.
ALCESTE. *(Sotto voce, to Philinte.)*
How can you say that? Why, the thing is frightful.
ORONTE.
You fair face smiled on me awhile,
But was it kindness so to enchant me?
'Twould have been fairer not to smile,
If hope was all you meant to grant me.
PHILINTE.
What a clever thought! How handsomely you phrase it!

23

ALCESTE. *(Sotto voce, to Philinte.)*
You know the thing is trash. How dare you praise it?
ORONTE.
If it's to be my passion's fate
Thus everlastingly to wait,
Then death will come to set me free:
For death is fairer than the fair;
Phyllis, to hope is to despair
When one must hope eternally.
PHILINTE.
The close is exquisite—full of feeling and grace.
ALCESTE. *(Sotto voce, aside.)*
Oh, blast the close; you'd better close your face
Before you send your lying soul to hell.
PHILINTE.
I can't remember a poem I've liked so well.
ALCESTE. *(Sotto voce, aside.)*
Good Lord!
ORONTE. *(To Philinte.)*
                I fear you're flattering me a bit.
PHILINTE.
Oh, no!
ALCESTE. *(Sotto voce, aside.)*
                What else d'you call it, you hypocrite?
ORONTE. *(To Alceste.)*
But you, Sir, keep your promise now: don't shrink
From telling me sincerely what you think.
ALCESTE.
Sir, these are delicate matters; we all desire
To be told that we've the true poetic fire.
But once, to one whose name I shall not mention,
I said, regarding some verse of his invention,
That gentlemen should rigorously control
That itch to write which often afflicts the soul;
That one should curb the heady inclination
To publicize one's little avocation;
And that in showing off one's works of art
One often plays a very clownish part.

ORONTE.
Are you suggesting in a devious way
That I ought not...
ALCESTE.

                       Oh, that I do not say.
Further, I told him that no fault is worse
Than that of writing frigid, lifeless verse,
And that the merest whisper of such a shame
Suffices to destroy a man's good name.
ORONTE.
D'you mean to say my sonnet's dull and trite?
ALCESTE.
I don't say that. But I went on to cite
Numerous cases of once-respected men
Who came to grief by taking up the pen.
ORONTE.
And am I like them? Do I write so poorly?
ALCESTE.
I don't say that. But I told this person, "Surely
You're under no necessity to compose;
Why you should wish to publish, heaven knows.
There's no excuse for printing tedious rot
Unless one writes for bread, as you do not.
Resist temptation, then, I beg of you;
Conceal your pastimes from the public view;
And don't give up, on any provocation,
Your present high and courtly reputation,
To purchase at a greedy printer's shop
The name of silly author and scribbling fop."
These were the points I tried to make him see.
ORONTE.
I sense that they are also aimed at me;
But now—about my sonnet—I'd like to be told...
ALCESTE.
Frankly, that sonnet should be pigeonholed.
You've chosen the worst models to imitate.

The style's unnatural. Let me illustrate:

For example, *Your fair face smiled on me awhile,*
Followed by, *'Twould have been fairer not to smile!*
Or this: *Such joy is full of rue;*
Or this: *For death is fairer than the fair;*
Or, *Phyllis, to hope is to despair*
    When one must hope eternally!

This artificial style, that's all the fashion,
Has neither taste, nor honesty, nor passion;
It's nothing but a sort of wordy play,
And nature never spoke in such a way.
What, in this shallow age, is not debased?
Our fathers, though less refined, had better taste:
I'd barter all that men admire today
For one old love-song I shall try to say:

> *If the King had given me for my own*
> *Paris, his citadel,*
> *And I for that must leave alone*
> *Her whom I love so well,*
> *I'd say then to the Crown,*
> *Take back your glittering town;*
> *My darling is more fair, I swear,*
> *My darling is more fair.*

The rhyme's not rich, the style is rough and old,
But don't you see that it's the purest gold
Beside the tinsel nonsense now preferred,
And that there's passion in its every word?

> *If the King had given me for my own*
> *Paris, his citadel,*
> *And I for that must leave alone*
> *Her whom I love so well,*

> *I'd say then to the Crown,*
> *Take back your glittering town;*
> *My darling is more fair, I swear,*
> *My darling is more fair.*

There speaks a loving heart. *(To Philinte.)* You're laughing, eh?
Laugh on, my precious wit. Whatever you say,
I hold that song's worth all the bibelots
That people hail today with ah's and oh's.
ORONTE.
And I maintain my sonnet's very good.
ALCESTE.
It's not at all surprising that you should.
You have your reasons; permit me to have mine
For thinking that you cannot write a line.
ORONTE.
Others have praised my sonnet to the skies.
ALCESTE.
I lack their art of telling pleasant lies.
ORONTE.
You seem to think you've got no end of wit.
ALCESTE.
To praise your verse, I'd need still more of it.
ORONTE.
I'm not in need of your approval, Sir.
ALCESTE.
That's good; you couldn't have it if you were.
ORONTE.
Come now, I'll lend you the subject of my sonnet;
I'd like to see you try to improve upon it.
ALCESTE.
I might, by chance, write something just as shoddy;
But then I wouldn't show it to everybody.
ORONTE.
You're most opinionated and conceited.

ALCESTE.
Go find your flatterers, and be better treated.
ORONTE. Look here, my little fellow, pray watch your tone.
ALCESTE.
My great big fellow, you'd better watch your own.
PHILINTE. *(Stepping between them.)*
Oh, please, please, gentlemen! This will never do.
ORONTE.
The fault is mine, and I leave the field to you.
I am your servant, Sir, in every way.
ALCESTE.
And I, Sir, am your most abject valet.

SCENE THREE

PHILINTE, ALCESTE

PHILINTE.
Well, as you see, sincerity in excess
Can get you into a very pretty mess;
Oronte was hungry for appreciation...
ALCESTE.
Don't speak to me.
PHILINTE.
     What?
ALCESTE.
       No more conversation.
PHILINTE.
Really, now...
ALCESTE.
     Leave me alone.
PHILINTE.
        If I...

ALCESTE.

Out of my sight!

PHILINTE.

But what...

ALCESTE.

I won't listen.

PHILINTE.

But...

ALCESTE.

Silence!

PHILINTE.

Now, is it polite...

ALCESTE.

By heaven, I've had enough. Don't follow me.

PHILINTE.

Ah, you're just joking. I'll keep you company.

ACT II
SCENE ONE

ALCESTE, CELIMENE

ALCESTE.
Shall I speak plainly, Madam? I confess
Your conduct gives me infinite distress,
And my resentment's grown too hot to smother.
Soon, I forsee, we'll break with one another.
If I said otherwise, I should deceive you;
Sooner or later, I shall be forced to leave you,
And if I swore that we shall never part,
I should misread the omens of my heart.
CELIMENE.
You kindly saw me home, it would appear,
So as to pour invectives in my ear.
ALCESTE.
I've no desire to quarrel. But I deplore
Your inability to shut the door
On all these suitors who beset you so.
There's what annoys me, if you care to know.
CELIMENE.
Is it my fault that all these men pursue me?
And I to blame if they're attracted to me?
And when they gently beg an audience,
Ought I to take a stick and drive them hence?
ALCESTE.
Madam, there's no necessity for a stick;
A less responsive heart would do the trick.
Of your attractiveness I don't complain;

But those your charms attract, you then detain
By a most melting and receptive manner,
And so enlist their hearts beneath your banner.
It's the agreeable hopes which you excite
That keep these lovers round you day and night;
Were they less liberally smiled upon,
That sighing troop would very soon be gone.
But tell me, Madam, why it is that lately
This man Clitandre interests you so greatly?
Because of what high merits do you deem
Him worthy of the honor of your esteem?
Is it that your admiring glances linger
On the splendidly long nail of his little finger?
Or do you share the general deep respect
For the blond wig he chooses to affect?
Are you in love with his embroidered hose?
Do you adore his ribbons and his bows?
Or is it that this paragon bewitches
Your tasteful eye with his vast German breeches?
Perhaps his giggle, or his falsetto voice,
Makes him the latest gallant of your choice?
CELIMENE.
You're much mistaken to resent him so.
Why I put up with him you surely know:
My lawsuit's very shortly to be tried,
And I must have his influence on my side.
ALCESTE.
Then lose your lawsuit, Madam, or let it drop;
Don't torture me by humoring such a fop.
CELIMENE.
You're jealous of the whole world, Sir.
ALCESTE.

                                    That's true,
Since the whole world is well-received by you.
CELIMENE.
That my good nature is so unconfined

Should serve to pacify your jealous mind;
Were I to smile on one, and scorn the rest,
Then you might have some cause to be distressed.
ALCESTE.
Well, if I mustn't be jealous, tell me, then,
Just how I'm better treated than other men.
CELIMENE.
You know you have my love. Will that not do?
ALCESTE.
What proof have I that what you say is true?
CELIMENE.
I would expect, Sir, that my having said it
Might give the statement a sufficient credit.
ALCESTE.
But how can I be sure that you don't tell
The selfsame thing to other men as well?
CELIMENE.
What a gallant speech! How flattering to me!
What a sweet creature you make me out to be!
Well then, to save you from the pangs of doubt,
All that I've said I hereby cancel out;
Now, none but yourself shall make a monkey of you:
Are you content?
ALCESTE.
                Why, why am I doomed to love you?
I swear that I shall bless the blissful hour
When this poor heart's no longer in your power!
I make no secret of it: I've done my best
To exorcise this passion from my breast;
But thus far all in vain; it will not go;
It's for my sins that I must love you so.
CELIMENE.
Your love for me is matchless, Sir; that's clear.
ALCESTE.
Indeed, in all the world it has no peer;
Words can't describe the nature of my passion,
And no man ever loved in such a fashion.

CELIMENE.
Yes, it's a brand-new fashion, I agree:
You show your love by castigating me,
And all your speeches are enraged and rude.
I've never been so furiously wooed.
ALCESTE.
Yet you could calm that fury, if you chose.
Come, shall we bring our quarrels to a close?
Let's speak with open hearts, then, and begin...

SCENE TWO

CELIMENE, ALCESTE, BASQUE

CELIMENE.
What is it?
BASQUE.

   Acaste is here.
CELIMENE.

      Well, send him in.

SCENE THREE

CELIMENE, ALCESTE

ALCESTE.
What! Shall we never be alone at all?
You're always ready to receive a call,
And you can't bear, for ten ticks of the clock,
Not to keep open house for all who knock.

CELIMENE.
I couldn't refuse him: he'd be most put out.
ALCESTE.
Surely that's not worth worrying about.
CELIMENE.
Acaste would never forgive me if he guessed
That I consider him a dreadful pest.
ALCESTE.
If he's a pest, why bother with him then?
CLITANDRE.
Heavens! One can't antagonize such men;
Why, they're the chartered gossips of the court,
And have a say in things of every sort.
One must receive them, and be full of charm;
They're no great help, but they can do you harm,
And though your influence be ever so great,
They're hardly the best people to alienate.
ALCESTE.
I see, dear lady, that you could make a case
For putting up with the whole human race;
These friendships that you calculate so nicely...

SCENE FOUR

ALCESTE, CELIMENE, BASQUE

BASQUE.
Madam, Clitandre is here as well.
ALCESTE.

                              Precisely.

CELIMENE.
Where are you going?

ALCESTE.
                    Elsewhere.
CELIMENE.
                              Stay.
ALCESTE.
                                        No, no.
CELIMENE.
Stay, Sir.
ALCESTE.
            I can't.
CELIMENE.
                    I wish it.
ALCESTE.
                              No, I must go.
I beg you, Madam, not to press the matter;
You know I have no taste for idle chatter.
CELIMENE.
Stay: I command you.
ALCESTE.
                    No, I cannot stay.
CELIMENE.
Very well; you have my leave to go away.

SCENE FIVE

ELIANTE,   PHILINTE,   ACASTE,   CLITANDRE,
ALCESTE, CELIMENE, BASQUE

ELIANTE. *(To Célimène.)*
The Marquesses have kindly come to call.
Were they announced?
CELIMENE.
                    Yes. Basque, bring chairs for all.

(Basque provides the chairs, and exits.)
(To Alceste.)
You haven't gone?
ALCESTE.

                 No; and I shan't depart
Till you decide who's foremost in your heart.
CELIMENE.
Oh, hush.
ALCESTE.

       It's time to choose; take them, or me.
CELIMENE.
You're mad.
ALCESTE.

         I'm not, as you shall shortly see.
CELIMENE.
Oh?
ALCESTE.
  You'll decide.
CELIMENE.

           You're joking now, dear friend.
ALCESTE.
No, no; you'll choose; my patience is at an end.
CLITANDRE.
Madam, I come from court, where poor Cléonte
Behaved like a perfect fool, as is his wont.
Has he no friend to counsel him, I wonder,
And teach him less unerringly to blunder?
CELIMENE.
It's true, the man's a most accomplished dunce;
His gauche behavior charms the eye at once;
And every time one sees him, on my word,
His manner's grown a trifle more absurd.
ACASTE.
Speaking of dunces, I've just now conversed
With old Damon, who's one of the very worst;
I stood a lifetime in the broiling sun
Before his dreary monologue was done.

36

CELIMENE.
Oh, he's a wondrous talker, and has the power
To tell you nothing hour after hour:
If, by mistake, he ever came to the point,
The shock would put his jawbone out of joint.
ELIANTE. *(To Philinte.)*
The conversation takes its usual turn,
And all our dear friends' ears will shortly burn.
CLITANDRE.
Timante's a character, Madam.
CELIMENE.
                              Isn't he, though?
A man of mystery from top to toe,
Who moves about in a romantic mist
On secret missions which do not exist.
His talk is full of eyebrows and grimaces;
How tired one gets of his momentous faces;
He's always whispering something confidential
Which turns out to be quite inconsequential;
Nothing's too slight for him to mystify;
He even whispers when he says "good-by."
ACASTE.
Tell us about Géralde.
CELIMENE.
                              That tiresome ass.
He mixes only with the titled class,
And fawns on dukes and princes, and is bored
With anyone who's not at least a lord.
The man's obsessed with rank, and his discourses
Are all of hounds and carriages and horses;
He uses Christian names with all the great,
And the word Milord, with him, is out of date.
CLITANDRE.
He's very taken with Bélise, I hear.
CELIMENE.
She is the dreariest company, poor dear.

Whenever she comes to call, I grope about
To find some topic which will draw her out,
But, owing to her dry and faint replies,
The conversation wilts, and droops, and dies.
In vain one hopes to animate her face
By mentioning the ultimate commonplace;
But sun or shower, even hail or frost
Are matters she can instantly exhaust.
Meanwhile her visit, painful though it is,
Drags on and on through mute eternities,
And though you ask the time, and yawn, and yawn,
She sits there like a stone and won't be gone.
ACASTE.
Now for Adraste.
CELIMENE.

           Oh, that conceited elf
Has a gigantic passion for himself;
He rails against the court, and cannot bear it
That none will recognize his hidden merit;
All honors given to others give offense
To his imaginary excellence.
CLITANDRE.
What about young Cléon? His house, they say,
Is full of the best society, night and day.
CELIMENE.
His cook has made him popular, not he:
It's Cléon's table that people come to see.
ELIANTE.
He gives a splendid dinner, you must admit.
CELIMENE.
But must he serve himself along with it?
For my taste, he's a most insipid dish
Whose presence sours the wine and spoils the fish.
PHILINTE.
Damis, his uncle, is admired no end.
What's your opinion, Madam?

CELIMENE.

                                    Why, he's my friend.
PHILINTE.
He seems a decent fellow, and rather clever.
CELIMENE.
He works too hard at cleverness, however.
I hate to see him sweat and struggle so
To fill his conversation with bon mots.
Since he's decided to become a wit
His taste's so pure that nothing pleases it;
He scolds at all the latest books and plays,
Thinking that wit must never stoop to praise,
That finding fault's a sign of intellect,
That all appreciation is abject,
And that by damning everything in sight
One shows oneself in a distinguished light.
He's scornful even of our conversations:
Their trivial nature sorely tries his patience;
He folds his arms, and stands above the battle,
And listens sadly to our childish prattle.
ACASTE.
Wonderful, Madam! You've hit him off precisely.
CLITANDRE.
No one can sketch a character so nicely.
ALCESTE.
How bravely, Sirs, you cut and thrust at all
These absent fools, till one by one they fall:
But let one come in sight, and you'll at once
Embrace the man you lately called a dunce,
Telling him in a tone sincere and fervent
How proud you are to be his humble servant.
CLITANDRE.
Why pick on us? Madame's been speaking, Sir,
And you should quarrel, if you must, with her.
ALCESTE.
No, no, by God, the fault is yours, because

You lead her on with laughter and applause,
And make her think that she's the more delightful
The more her talk is scandalous and spiteful.
Oh, she would stoop to malice far, far less
If no such claque approved her cleverness.
It's flatterers like you whose foolish praise
Nourishes all the vices of these days.
PHILINTE.
But why protest when someone ridicules
Those you'd condemn, yourself, as knaves or fools?
CELIMENE.
Why, Sir? Because he loves to make a fuss.
You don't expect him to agree with us,
When there's an opportunity to express
His heaven-sent spirit of contrariness?
What other people think, he can't abide;
Whatever they say, he's on the other side;
He lives in deadly terror of agreeing;
'Twould make him seem an ordinary being.
Indeed, he's so in love with contradiction,
He'll turn against his most profound conviction
And with a furious eloquence deplore it,
If only someone else is speaking for it.
ALCESTE.
Go on, dear lady, mock me as you please;
You have your audience in ecstasies.
PHILINTE.
But what she says is true: you have a way
Of bridling at whatever people say;
Whether they praise or blame, your angry spirit
Is equally unsatisfied to hear it.
ALCESTE.
Men, Sir, are always wrong, and that's the reason
That righteous anger's never out of season;
All that I hear in all their conversation
Is flattering praise or reckless condemnation.

CELIMENE.
But...
ALCESTE.
No, no, Madam, I am forced to state
That you have pleasures which I deprecate,
And that these others, here, are much to blame
For nourishing the faults which are your shame.
CLITANDRE.
I shan't defend myself, Sir; but I vow
I'd thought this lady faultless until now.
ACASTE.
I see her charms and graces, which are many;
But as for faults, I've never noticed any.
ALCESTE.
I see them, Sir; and rather than ignore them,
I strenuously criticize her for them.
The more one loves, the more one should object
To every blemish, every least defect.
Were I this lady, I would soon get rid
Of lovers who approved of all I did,
And by their slack indulgence and applause
Endorsed my follies and excused my flaws.
CELIMENE.
If all hearts beat according to your measure,
The dawn of love would be the end of pleasure;
And love would find its perfect consummation
In ecstasies of rage and reprobation.
ELIANTE.
Love, as a rule, affects men otherwise,
And lovers rarely love to criticize.
They see their lady as a charming blur,
And find all things commendable in her.
If she has any blemish, fault, or shame,
They will redeem it by a pleasing name.
The pale-faced lady's lily-white, perforce;
The swarthy one's a sweet brunette, of course;

The spindly lady has a slender grace;
The fat one has a most majestic pace;
The plain one, with her dress in disarray,
They classify as *beauté negligée;*
The hulking one's a goddess in their eyes,
The dwarf, a concentrate of Paradise;
The haughty lady has a noble mind;
The mean one's witty, and the dull one's kind;
The chatterbox has liveliness and verve,
The mute one has a virtuous reserve.
So lovers manage, in their passion's cause,
To love their ladies even for their flaws.
ALCESTE.
But I still say...
CELIMENE.

                I think it would be nice
To stroll around the gallery once or twice.
What! You're not going, Sirs?
CLITANDRE and ACASTE.

                  No, Madam, no.
ALCESTE.
You seem to be in terror lest they go.
Do what you will, Sirs; leave, or linger on,
But I shan't go till after you are gone.
ACASTE.
I'm free to linger, unless I should perceive
Madame is tired, and wishes me to leave.
CLITANDRE.
And as for me, I needn't go today
Until the hour of the King's *coucher.*
CELIMENE. *(To Alceste.)*
You're joking, surely?
ALCESTE.

              Not in the least; we'll see
Whether you'd rather part with them, or me.

SCENE SIX

BASQUE. *(To Alceste.)*
Sir, there's a fellow here who bids me state
That he must see you, and that it can't wait.
ALCESTE.
Tell him that I have no such pressing affairs.
BASQUE.
It's a long tailcoat that this fellow wears,
With gold all over.
CELIMENE. *(To Alceste.)*
               You'd best go down and see.
Or—have him enter.

SCENE SEVEN

ALCESTE, CELIMENE, ELIANTE, ACASTE, PHILINTE, CLITANDRE, A GUARD of the Marshalsea

ALCESTE. *(Confronting the guard.)*
               Well, what do you want with me?
Come in, Sir.
GUARD.
            I've a word, Sir, for your ear.

ALCESTE.
Speak it aloud, Sir; I shall strive to hear.
GUARD.
The Marshals have instructed me to say
You must report to them without delay.
ALCESTE.
Who? Me, Sir?
GUARD.
                    Yes, Sir; you.
ALCESTE.
                                    But what do they want?
PHILINTE. *(To Alceste.)*
To scotch your silly quarrel with Oronte.
CELIMENE. *(To Philinte.)*
What quarrel?
PHILINTE.
                    Oronte and he have fallen out
Over some verse he spoke his mind about;
The Marshals wish to arbitrate the matter.
ALCESTE.
Never shall I equivocate or flatter!
PHILINTE.
You'd best obey their summons; come, let's go.
ALCESTE.
How can they mend our quarrel, I'd like to know?
Am I to make a cowardly retraction,
And praise those jingles to his satisfaction?
I'll not recant; I've judged that sonnet rightly.
It's bad.
PHILINTE.
                    But you might say so more politely...
ALCESTE.
I'll not back down; his verses make me sick.
PHILINTE.
If only you could be more politic!
But come, let's go.

ALCESTE.

                    I'll go, but I won't unsay
A single word.
PHILINTE.

                    Well, let's be on our way.
ALCESTE.
Till I am ordered by my lord the King
To praise that poem, I shall say the thing
Is scandalous, by God, and that the poet
Ought to be hanged for having the nerve to show it.
(To Clitandre and Acaste, who are laughing.)
By heaven, Sirs, I really didn't know
That I was being humorous.
CELIMENE.

                         Go, Sir, go;
Settle your business.
ALCESTE.

                    I shall, and when I'm through,
I shall return to settle things with you.

ACT III
SCENE ONE

CLITANDRE, ACASTE

CLITANDRE.
Dear Marquess, how contented you appear;
All things delight you, nothing mars your cheer.
Can you, in perfect honesty, declare
That you've a right to be so debonair?
ACASTE.
By Jove, when I survey myself, I find
No cause whatever for distress of mind.
I'm young and rich; I can in modesty
Lay claim to an exalted pedigree;
And owing to my name and my condition
I shall not want for honors and position.
Then as to courage, that most precious trait,
I seem to have it, as was proved of late
Upon the field of honor, where my bearing,
They say, was very cool and rather daring.
I've wit, of course; and taste in such perfection
That I can judge without the least reflection,
And at the theater, which is my delight,
Can make or break a play on opening night,
And lead the crowd in hisses or bravos,
And generally be known as one who knows.
I'm clever, handsome, gracefully polite;
My waist is small, my teeth are strong and white;
As for my dress, the world's astonished eyes
Assure me that I bear away the prize.

I find myself in favor everywhere,
Honored by men, and worshiped by the fair;
And since these things are so, it seems to me
I'm justified in my complacency.
CLITANDRE.
Well, if so many ladies hold you dear,
Why do you press a hopeless courtship here?
ACASTE.
Hopeless, you say? I'm not the sort of fool
That likes his ladies difficult and cool.
Men who are awkward, shy, and peasantish
May pine for heartless beauties, if they wish,
Grovel before them, bear their cruelties,
Woo them with tears and sighs and bended knees,
And hope by dogged faithfulness to gain
What their poor merits never could obtain.
For men like me, however, it makes no sense
To love on trust, and foot the whole expense.
Whatever any lady's merits be,
I think, thank God, that I'm as choice as she;
That if my heart is kind enough to burn
For her, she owes me something in return;
And that in any proper love affair
The partners must invest an equal share.
CLITANDRE.
You think, then, that our hostess favors you?
ACASTE.
I've reason to believe that that is true.
CLITANDRE.
How did you come to such a mad conclusion?
You're blind, dear fellow. This is sheer delusion.
ACASTE.
All right, then: I'm deluded and I'm blind.
CLITANDRE.
Whatever put the notion in your mind?
ACASTE.
Delusion.

CLITANDRE.
              What persuades you that you're right?
ACASTE.
I'm blind.
CLITANDRE.
              But have you any proofs to cite?
ACASTE.
I tell you I'm deluded.
CLITANDRE.
                              Have you, then,
Received some secret pledge from Célimène?
ACASTE.
Oh, no: she scorns me.
CLITANDRE.
                              Tell me the truth, I beg.
ACASTE.
She just can't bear me.
CLITANDRE.
                              Ah, don't pull my leg.
Tell me what hope she's given you, I pray.
ACASTE.
I'm hopeless, and it's you who win the day.
She hates me thoroughly, and I'm so vexed
I mean to hang myself on Tuesday next.
CLITANDRE.
Dear Marquess, let us have an armistice
And make a treaty. What do you say to this?
If ever one of us can plainly prove
That Célimène encourages his love,
The other must abandon hope, and yield,
And leave him in possession of the field.
ACASTE.
Now, there's a bargain that appeals to me;
With all my heart, dear Marquess, I agree.
But hush.

SCENE TWO

CELIMENE, ACASTE, CLITANDRE

CELIMENE.
Still here?
CLITANDRE.
T'was love that stayed our feet.
CELIMENE.
I think I heard a carriage in the street.
Whose is it? D'you know?

SCENE THREE

CELIMENE, ACASTE, CLITANDRE, BASQUE

BASQUE.
Arsinoé is here,
Madame.
CELIMENE.
Arsinoé, you say? Oh, dear.
BASQUE.
Eliante is entertaining her below.
CELIMENE.
What brings the creature here, I'd like to know?
ACASTE.
They say she's dreadfully prudish, but in fact
I think her piety...

CELIMENE.
                    It's all an act.
At heart she's worldly, and her poor success
In snaring men explains her prudishness.
It breaks her heart to see the beaux and gallants
Engrossed by other women's charms and talents,
And so she's always in a jealous rage
Against the faulty standards of the age.
She lets the world believe that she's a prude
To justify her loveless solitude,
And strives to put a brand of moral shame
On all the graces that she cannot claim.
But still she'd love a lover; and Alceste
Appears to be the one she'd love the best.
His visits here are poison to her pride;
She seems to think I've lured him from her side;
And everywhere, at court or in the town,
The spiteful, envious woman runs me down.
In short, she's just as stupid as can be,
Vicious and arrogant in the last degree,
And...

SCENE FOUR

ARSINOE, CELIMENE, CLITANDRE, ACASTE

CELIMENE.
          Ah! What happy chance has brought you here?
I've thought about you ever so much, my dear.
ARSINOE.
I've come to tell you something you should know.
CELIMENE.
How good of you to think of doing so!
(Clitandre and Acaste go out, laughing.)

SCENE FIVE

ARSINOE, CELIMENE

ARSINOE.
It's just as well those gentlemen didn't tarry.
CELIMENE.
Shall we sit down?
ARSINOE.
                    That won't be necessary.
Madam, the flame of friendship ought to burn
Brightest in matters of the most concern,
And as there's nothing which concerns us more
Than honor, I have hastened to your door
To bring you, as your friend, some information
About the status of your reputation.
I visited, last night, some virtuous folk,
And, quite by chance, it was of you they spoke;
There was, I fear, no tendency to praise
Your light behavior and your dashing ways.
The quantity of gentlemen you see
And your by now notorious coquetry
Were both so vehemently criticized
By everyone, that I was much surprised.
Of course, I needn't tell you where I stood;
I came to your defense as best I could,
Assured them you were harmless, and declared
Your soul was absolutely unimpaired.
But there are some things, you must realize,
One can't excuse, however hard one tries,
And I was forced at last into conceding

That your behavior, Madam, is misleading,
That it makes a bad impression, giving rise
To ugly gossip and obscene surmise,
And that if you were more *overtly* good,
You wouldn't be so much misunderstood.
Not that I think you've been unchaste—no! no!
The saints preserve me from a thought so low!
But mere good conscience never did suffice:
One must avoid the outward show of vice.
Madam, you're too intelligent, I'm sure.
To think my motives anything but pure
In offering you this counsel—which I do
Out of a zealous interest in you.
CELIMENE.
Madam, I haven't taken you amiss;
I'm very much obliged to you for this;
And I'll at once discharge the obligation
By telling you about *your* reputation.
You've been so friendly as to let me know
What certain people say of me, and so
I mean to follow your benign example
By offering you a somewhat similar sample.
The other day, I went to an affair
And found some most distinguished people there
Discussing piety, both false and true.
The conversation soon came round to you.
Alas! Your prudery and bustling zeal
Appeared to have a very slight appeal.
Your affectation of a grave demeanor,
Your endless talk of virtue and of honor,
The aptitude of your suspicious mind
For finding sin where there is none to find,
Your towering self-esteem, that pitying face
With which you contemplate the human race,
Your sermonizings and your sharp aspersions
On people's pure and innocent diversions—

All these were mentioned, Madam, and, in fact,
Were roundly and concertedly attacked.
"What good," they said, "are all these outward shows,
When everything belies her pious pose?
She prays incessantly; but then, they say,
She beats her maids and cheats them of their pay;
She shows her zeal in every holy place,
But still she's vain enough to paint her face;
She holds that naked statues are immoral,
But with a naked *man* she'd have no quarrel."
Of course, I said to everybody there
That they were being viciously unfair;
But still they were disposed to criticize you,
And all agreed that someone should advise you
To leave the morals of the world alone,
And worry rather more about your own.
They felt that one's self-knowledge should be great
Before one thinks of setting others straight;
That one should learn the art of living well
Before one threatens other men with hell,
And that the Church is best equipped, no doubt,
To guide our souls and root our vices out.
Madam, you're too intelligent, I'm sure,
To think my motives anything but pure
In offering you this counsel—which I do
Out of a zealous interest in you.
ARSINOE.
I dared not hope for gratitude, but I
Did not expect so acid a reply;
I judge, since you've been so extremely tart,
That my good counsel pierced you to the heart.
CELIMENE.
Far from it, Madam. Indeed, it seems to me
We ought to trade advice more frequently.
One's vision of oneself is so defective
That it would be an excellent corrective.
If you are willing, Madam, let's arrange

Shortly to have another frank exchange
In which we'll tell each other, *entre nous,*
What you've heard tell of me, and I of you.
ARSINOE.
Oh, people never censure you, my dear;
It's me they criticize. Or so I hear.
CELIMENE.
Madam, I think we either blame or praise
According to our taste and length of days.
There is a time of life for coquetry,
And there's a season, too, for prudery.
When all one's charms are gone, it is, I'm sure,
Good strategy to be devout and pure:
It makes one seem a little less forsaken.
Some day, perhaps, I'll take the road you've taken:
Time brings all things. But I have time aplenty,
And see no cause to be a prude at twenty.
ARSINOE.
You give your age in such a gloating tone
That one would think I was an ancient crone;
We're not so far apart, in sober truth,
That you can mock me with a boast of youth!
Madam, you baffle me. I wish I knew
What moves you to provoke me as you do.
CELIMENE.
For my part, Madam, I should like to know
Why you abuse me everywhere you go.
Is it my fault, dear lady, that your hand
Is not, alas, in very great demand?
If men admire me, if they pay me court
And daily make me offers of the sort
You'd dearly love to have them make to you,
How can I help it? What would you have me do?
If what you want is lovers, please feel free
To take as many as you can from me.

ARSINOE.
Oh, come. D'you think the world is losing sleep
Over that flock of lovers which you keep,
Or that we find it difficult to guess
What price you pay for their devotedness?
Surely you don't expect us to suppose
Mere merit could attract so many beaux?
It's not your virtue that they're dazzled by;
Nor is it virtuous love for which they sigh.
You're fooling no one, Madam; the world's not blind;
There's many a lady heaven has designed
To call men's noblest, tenderest feelings out,
Who has no lovers dogging her about;
From which it's plain that lovers nowadays
Must be acquired in bold and shameless ways,
And only pay one court for such reward
As modesty and virtue can't afford.
Then don't be quite so puffed up, if you please,
About your tawdry little victories;
Try, if you can, to be a shade less vain,
And treat the world with somewhat less disdain.
If one were envious of your amours,
One soon could have a following like yours;
Lovers are no great trouble to collect
If one prefers them to one's self-respect.
CELIMENE.
Collect them then, my dear; I'd love to see
You demonstrate that charming theory;
Who knows, you might...
ARSINOE.
                Now, Madam, that will do;
It's time to end this trying interview.
My coach is late in coming to your door,
Or I'd have taken leave of you before.
CELIMENE.
Oh, please don't feel that you must rush away;

I'd be delighted, Madam, if you'd stay.
However, lest my conversation bore you,
Let me provide some better company for you;
This gentleman, who comes most apropos,
Will please you more than I could do, I know.

SCENE SIX

ALCESTE, CELIMENE, ARSINOE

CELIMENE.
Alceste, I have a little note to write
Which simply must go out before tonight;
Please entertain *Madame;* I'm sure that she
Will overlook my incivility.

SCENE SEVEN

ALCESTE, ARSINOE

ARSINOE.
Well, Sir, our hostess graciously contrives
For us to chat until my coach arrives;
And I shall be forever in her debt
For granting me this little tête-à-tête.
We women very rightly give our hearts
To men of noble character and parts,
And your especial merits, dear Alceste,
Have roused the deepest sympathy in my breast.
Oh, how I wish they had sufficent sense
At court, to recognize your excellence!

They wrong you greatly, Sir. How it must hurt you
Never to be rewarded for your virtue!
ALCESTE.
Why, Madam, what cause have I to feel aggrieved?
What great and brilliant thing have I achieved?
What service have I rendered to the King
That I should look to him for anything?
ARSINOE.
Not everyone who's honored by the State
Has done great services. A man must wait
Till time and fortune offer him the chance.
Your merit, Sir, is obvious at a glance,
And...
ALCESTE.
   Ah, forget my merit; I'm not neglected.
The court, I think, can hardly be expected
To mine men's souls for merit, and unearth
Our hidden virtues and our secret worth.
ARSINOE.
Some virtues, though, are far too bright to hide;
Yours are acknowledged, Sir, on every side.
Indeed, I've heard you warmly praised of late
By persons of considerable weight.
ALCESTE.
This fawning age has praise for everyone,
And all distinctions, Madam, are undone.
All things have equal honor nowadays,
And no one should be gratified by praise.
To be admired, one only need exist,
And every lackey's on the honors list.
ARSINOE.
I only wish, Sir, that you had your eye
On some position at court, however high;
You'd only have to hint at such a notion
For me to set the proper wheels in motion;
I've certain friendships I'd be glad to use
To get you any office you might choose.

ALCESTE.
Madam, I fear that any such ambition
Is wholly foreign to my disposition.
The soul God gave me isn't of the sort
That prospers in the weather of a court.
It's all too obvious that I don't possess
The virtues necessary for success.
My one great talent is for speaking plain;
I've never learned to flatter or to feign;
And anyone so stupidly sincere
Had best not seek a courtier's career.
Outside the court, I know, one must dispense
With honors, privilege, and influence;
But still one gains the right, foregoing these,
Not to be tortured by the wish to please.
One needn't live in dread of snubs and slights,
Nor praise the verse that every idiot writes,
Nor humor silly Marquesses, nor bestow
Politic sighs on Madam So-and-So.
ARSINOE.
Forget the court, then; let the matter rest.
But I've another cause to be distressed
About your present situation, Sir.
It's to your love affair that I refer.
She whom you love, and who pretends to love you,
Is, I regret to say, unworthy of you.
ALCESTE.
Why, Madam! Can you seriously intend
To make so grave a charge against your friend?
ARSINOE.
Alas, I must. I've stood aside too long
And let that lady do you grievous wrong;
But now my debt to conscience shall be paid;
I tell you that your love has been betrayed.
ALCESTE.
I thank you, Madam; you're extremely kind.
Such words are soothing to a lover's mind.

ARSINOE.
Yes, though she *is* my friend, I say again
You're very much too good for Célimène.
She's wantonly misled you from the start.
ALCESTE.
You may be right; who knows another's heart?
But ask yourself if it's the part of charity
To shake my soul with doubts of her sincerity.
ARSINOE.
Well, if you'd rather be a dupe than doubt her,
That's your affair. I'll say no more about her.
ALCESTE.
Madam, you know that doubt and vague suspicion
Are painful to a man in my position;
It's most unkind to worry me this way
Unless you've some real proof of what you say.
ARSINOE.
Sir, say no more: all doubt shall be removed,
And all that I've been saying shall be proved.
You've only to escort me home, and there
We'll look into the heart of this affair.
I've ocular evidence which will persuade you
Beyond a doubt, that Célimène's betrayed you.
Then, if you're saddened by that revelation,
Perhaps I can provide some consolation.

ACT IV
SCENE ONE

ELIANTE, PHILINTE

PHILINTE.
Madam, he acted like a stubborn child;
I thought they never would be reconciled;
In vain we reasoned, threatened, and appealed;
He stood his ground and simply would not yield.
The Marshals, I feel sure, have never heard
An argument so splendidly absurd.
"No, gentlemen," said he, "I'll not retract.
His verse is bad: extremely bad, in fact.
Surely it does the man no harm to know it.
Does it disgrace him, not to be a poet?
A gentleman may be respected still,
Whether he writes a sonnet well or ill.
That I dislike his verse should not offend him;
In all that touches honor, I commend him;
He's noble, brave, and virtuous—but I fear
He can't in truth be called a sonneteer.
I'll gladly praise his wardrobe; I'll endorse
His dancing, or the way he sits a horse;
But, gentlemen, I cannot praise his rhyme.
In fact, it ought to be a capital crime
For anyone so sadly unendowed
To write a sonnet, and read the thing aloud."
At length he fell into a gentler mood
And, striking a concessive attitude,

He paid Oronte the following courtesies:
"Sir, I regret that I'm so hard to please,
And I'm profoundly sorry that your lyric
Failed to provoke me to a panegyric."
After these curious words, the two embraced,
And then the hearing was adjourned—in haste.
ELIANTE.
His conduct has been very singular lately;
Still, I confess that I respect him greatly.
The honesty in which he takes such pride
Has—to my mind—its noble, heroic side.
In this false age, such candor seems outrageous;
But I could wish that it were more contagious.
PHILINTE.
What most intrigues me in our friend Alceste
Is the grand passion that rages in his breast.
The sullen humors he's compounded of
Should not, I think, dispose his heart to love;
But since they do, it puzzles me still more
That he should choose your cousin to adore.
ELIANTE.
It does, indeed, belie the theory
That love is born of gentle sympathy,
And that the tender passion must be based
On sweet accords of temper and of taste.
PHILINTE.
Does she return his love, do you suppose?
ELIANTE.
Ah, that'a difficult question, Sir. Who knows?
How can we judge the truth of her devotion?
Her heart's a stranger to its own emotion.
Sometimes it thinks it loves, when no love's there;
At other times it loves quite unaware.
PHILINTE.
I rather think Alceste is in for more
Distress and sorrow than he's bargained for;

Were he of my mind, Madam, his affection
Would turn in quite a different direction,
And we would see him more responsive to
The kind regard which receives from you.
ELIANTE.
Sir, I believe in frankness, and I'm inclined,
In matters of the heart, to speak my mind.
I don't oppose his love for her; indeed,
I hope with all my heart that he'll succeed,
And were it in my power, I'd rejoice
In giving him the lady of his choice.
But if, as happens frequently enough
In love affairs, he meets with a rebuff—
If Célimène should grant some rival's suit—
I'd gladly play the role of substitute;
Nor would his tender speeches please me less
Because they'd once been made without success.
PHILINTE.
Well, Madam, as for me, I don't oppose
Your hopes in this affair; and heaven knows
That in my conversations with the man
I plead your cause as often as I can.
But if those two should marry, and so remove
All chance that he will offer you his love,
Then I'll declare my own, and hope to see
Your gracious favor pass from him to me.
In short, should you be cheated of Alceste,
I'd be most happy to be second best.
ELIANTE.
Philinte, you're teasing.
PHILINTE.

                       Ah, Madam, never fear;
No words of mine were ever so sincere,
And I shall live in fretful expectation
Till I can make a fuller declaration.

SCENE TWO

ALCESTE, ELIANTE, PHILINTE

ALCESTE.
Avenge me, Madam! I must have satisfaction,
Or this great wrong will drive me to distraction!
ELIANTE.
Why, what's the matter? What's upset you so?
ALCESTE.
Madam, I've had a mortal, mortal blow.
If Chaos repossessed the universe,
I swear I'd not be shaken any worse.
I'm ruined...I can say no more...My soul...
ELIANTE.
Do try, Sir, to regain your self-control.
ALCESTE.
Just heaven! Why were so much beauty and grace
Bestowed on one so vicious and so base?
ELIANTE.
Once more, Sir, tell us...
ALCESTE.
　　　　　　　　My world has gone to wrack;
I'm—I'm betrayed; she's stabbed me in the back:
Yes, Célimène (who would have thought it of her?)
Is false to me, and has another lover.
ELIANTE.
Are you quite certain? Can you prove these things?
PHILINTE.
Lovers are prey to wild imaginings
And jealous fancies. No doubt there's some mistake...

ALCESTE.
Mind your own business, Sir, for heaven's sake.
(To Eliante.)
Madam, I have the proof that you demand
Here in my pocket, penned by her own hand.
Yes, all the shameful evidence one could want
Lies in this letter written to Oronte—
Oronte! whom I felt sure she couldn't love,
And hardly bothered to be jealous of.
PHILINTE.
Still, in a letter, appearances may deceive;
This may not be so bad as you believe.
ALCESTE.
Once more I beg you, Sir, to let me be;
Tend to your own affairs; leave mine to me.
ELIANTE.
Compose yourself; this anguish that you feel...
ALCESTE.
Is something, Madam, you alone can heal.
My outraged heart, beside itself with grief,
Appeals to you for comfort and relief.
Avenge me on your cousin, whose unjust
And faithless nature has deceived my trust;
Avenge a crime your pure soul must detest.
ELIANTE.
But how, Sir?
ALCESTE.
                    Madam, this heart within my breast
Is yours; pray take it; redeem my heart from her,
And so avenge me on my torturer.
Let her be punished by the fond emotion,
The ardent love, the bottomless devotion,
The faithful worship which this heart of mine
Will offer up to yours as to a shrine.
ELIANTE.
You have my sympathy, Sir, in all you suffer;
Nor do I scorn the noble heart you offer;

But I suspect you'll soon be mollified,
And this desire for vengeance will subside.
When some beloved hand has done us wrong
We thirst for retribution—but not for long;
However dark the deed that she's committed,
A lovely culprit's very soon acquitted.
Nothing's so stormy as an injured lover,
And yet no storm so quickly passes over.
ALCESTE.
No, Madam, no—this is no lovers' spat;
I'll not forgive her; it's gone too far for that;
My mind's made up; I'll kill myself before
I waste my hopes upon her any more.
Ah, here she is. My wrath intensifies.
I shall confront her with her tricks and lies,
And crush her utterly, and bring you then
A heart no longer slave to Célimène.

SCENE THREE

CELIMENE, ALCESTE

ALCESTE. *(Aside.)*
Sweet heaven, help me to control my passion.
CELIMENE. *(Initially aside, then to Alceste.)*
Oh, Lord. Why stand there staring in that fashion?
And what d'you mean by those dramatic sighs,
And that malignant glitter in your eyes?
ALCESTE.
I mean that sins which cause the blood to freeze
Look innocent beside your treacheries;
That nothing Hell's or Heaven's wrath could do
Ever produced so bad a thing as you.

CELIMENE.
Your compliments were always sweet and pretty.
ALCESTE.
Madam, it's not the moment to be witty.
No, blush and hang your head; you've ample reason,
Since I've the fullest evidence of your treason.
Ah, this is what my sad heart prophesied;
Now all my anxious fears are verified;
My dark suspicion and my gloomy doubt
Divined the truth, and now the truth is out.
For all your trickery, I was not deceived;
It was my bitter stars that I believed.
But don't imagine that you'll go scot-free;
You shan't misuse me with impunity.
I know that love's irrational and blind;
I know the heart's not subject to the mind,
And can't be reasoned into beating faster;
I know each soul is free to choose its master;
Therefore had you but spoken from the heart,
Rejecting my attentions from the start,
I'd have no grievance, or at any rate
I could complain of nothing but my fate.
Ah, but so falsely to encourage me—
That was a treason and a treachery
For which you cannot suffer too severely,
And you shall pay for that behavior dearly.
Yes, now I have no pity, not a shred;
My temper's out of hand; I've lost my head;
Shocked by the knowledge of your double-dealings,
My reason can't restrain my savage feelings;
A righteous wrath deprives me of my senses,
And I won't answer for the consequences.
CELIMENE.
What does this outburst mean? Will you please explain?
Have you, by any chance, gone quite insane?

ALCESTE.
Yes, yes, I went insane the day I fell
A victim to your black and fatal spell,
Thinking to meet with some sincerity
Among the treacherous charms that beckoned me.
CELIMENE.
Pooh. Of what treachery can you complain?
ALCESTE.
How sly you are, how cleverly you feign!
But you'll not victimize me any more.
Look: here's a document you've seen before.
This evidence, which I acquired today,
Leaves you, I think without a thing to say.
CELIMENE.
Is this what sent you into such a fit?
ALCESTE.
You should be blushing at the sight of it.
CELIMENE.
Ought I to blush? I truly don't see why.
ALCESTE.
Ah, now you're being bold as well as sly;
Since there's no signature, perhaps you'll claim...
CELIMENE.
I wrote it, whether or not it bears my name.
ALCESTE.
And you can view with equanimity
This proof of your disloyalty to me!
CELIMENE.
Oh, don't be so outrageous and extreme.
ALCESTE.
You take this matter lightly, it would seem.
Was it no wrong to me, no shame to you,
That you should send Oronte this billet-doux?
CELIMENE.
Oronte! Who said it was for him?

ALCESTE.

                                    Why, those
Who brought me this example of your prose.
But what's the difference? If you wrote the letter
To someone else, it pleases me no better.
My grievance and your guilt remain the same.
CELIMENE.
But need you rage, and need I blush for shame,
If this was written to a *woman* friend?
ALCESTE.
Ah! Most ingenious. I'm impressed no end;
And after that incredible evasion
Your guilt is clear. I need no more persuasion.
How dare you try so clumsy a deception?
D'you think I'm wholly wanting in perception?
Come, come, let's see how brazenly you'll try
To bolster up so palpable a lie:
Kindly construe this ardent closing section
As nothing more than sisterly affection!
Here, let me read it. Tell me, if you dare to,
That this is for a woman...
CELIMENE.

                                    I don't care to.
What right have you to badger and berate me,
And so highhandedly interrogate me?
ALCESTE.
Now, don't be angry; all I ask of you
Is that you justify a phrase or two...
CELIMENE.
No, I shall not. I utterly refuse,
And you may take those phrases as you choose.
ALCESTE.
Just show me how this letter could be meant
For a woman's eyes, and I shall be content.
CELIMENE.
No, no, it's for Oronte; you're perfectly right.

I welcome his attentions with delight,
I prize his character and his intellect,
And everything is just as you suspect.
Come, do your worst now; give your rage free rein;
But kindly cease to bicker and complain.
ALCESTE. *(Aside.)*
Good God! Could anything be more inhuman?
Was ever a heart so mangled by a woman?
When I complain of how she has betrayed me,
She bridles, and commences to upbraid me!
She tries my tortured patience to the limit;
She won't deny her guilt; she glories in it!
And yet my heart's too faint and cowardly
To break these chains of passion, and be free,
To scorn her as it should, and rise above
This unrewarded, mad, and bitter love.
(To Célimène.)
Ah, traitress, in how confident a fashion
You take advantage of my helpless passion,
And use my weakness for your faithless charms
To make me once again throw down my arms!
But do at least deny this black transgression;
Take back that mocking and perverse confession;
Defend this letter and your innocence,
And I, poor fool, will aid in your defense.
Pretend, pretend, that you are just and true,
And I shall make myself believe in you.
CELIMENE.
Oh, stop it. Don't be such a jealous dunce,
Or I shall leave off loving you at once.
Just why should I *pretend?* What could impel me
To stoop so low as that? And kindly tell me
Why, if I loved another, I shouldn't merely
Inform you of it, simply and sincerely!
I've told you where you stand, and that admission
Should altogether clear me of suspicion;

69

After so generous a guarantee,
What right have you to harbor doubts of me?
Since women are (from natural reticence)
Reluctant to declare their sentiments,
And since the honor of our sex requires
That we conceal our amorous desires,
Ought any man for whom such laws are broken
To question what the oracle has spoken?
Should he not rather feel an obligation
To trust that most obliging declaration?
Enough, now. Your suspicions quite disgust me;
Why should I love a man who doesn't trust me?
I cannot understand why I continue,
Fool that I am, to take an interest in you.
I ought to choose a man less prone to doubt,
And give you something to be vexed about.
ALCESTE.
Ah, what a poor enchanted fool I am;
These gentle words, no doubt, were all a sham;
But destiny requires me to entrust
My happiness to you, and so I must.
I'll love you to the bitter end, and see
How false and treacherous you dare to be.
CELIMENE.
No, you don't really love me as you ought.
ALCESTE.
I love you more than can be said or thought;
Indeed, I wish you were in such distress
That I might show my deep devotedness.
Yes, I could wish that you were wretchedly poor,
Unloved, uncherished, utterly obscure;
That fate had set you down upon the earth
Without possessions, rank, or gentle birth;
Then, by the offer of my heart, I might
Repair the great injustice of your plight;
I'd raise you from the dust, and proudly prove
The purity and vastness of my love.

CELIMENE.
This is a strange benevolence indeed!
God grant that I may never be in need...
Ah, here's Monsieur Dubois, in quaint disguise.

SCENE FOUR

CELIMENE, ALCESTE, DUBOIS

ALCESTE.
Well, why this costume? Why those frightened eyes?
What ails you?
DUBOIS.

             Well, Sir, things are most mysterious.
ALCESTE.
What do you mean?
DUBOIS.

                    I fear they're very serious.
ALCESTE.
What?
DUBOIS.

        Shall I speak more loudly?
ALCESTE.

                         Yes; speak out.
DUBOIS.
Isn't there someone here, Sir?
ALCESTE.

                      Speak, you lout!
Stop wasting time.
DUBOIS.

               Sir, we must slip away.
ALCESTE.
How's that?

DUBOIS.

          We must decamp without delay.

ALCESTE.

Explain yourself.

DUBOIS.

                I tell you we must fly.

ALCESTE.

What for?

DUBOIS.

        We mustn't pause to say good-by.

ALCESTE.

Now what d'you mean by all of this, you clown?

DUBOIS.

I mean, Sir, that we've got to leave this town.

ALCESTE.

I'll tear you limb from limb and joint from joint
If you don't come more quickly to the point.

DUBOIS.

Well, Sir, today a man in a black suit,
Who wore a black and ugly scowl to boot,
Left us a document scrawled in such a hand
As even Satan couldn't understand.
It bears upon your lawsuit, I don't doubt;
But all hell's devils couldn't make it out.

ALCESTE.

Well, well, go on. What then? I fail to see
How this event obliges us to flee.

DUBOIS.

Well, Sir: an hour later, hardly more,
A gentleman who's often called before
Came looking for you in an anxious way.
Not finding you, he asked me to convey
(Knowing I could be trusted with the same)
The following message...Now, what *was* his name?

ALCESTE.

Forget his name, you idiot. What did he say?

72

DUBOIS.
Well, it was one of your friends, Sir, anyway.
He warned you to begone, and he suggested
That if you stay, you may well be arrested.
ALCESTE.
What? Nothing more specific? Think, man, think!
DUBOIS.
No, Sir. He had me bring him pen and ink,
And dashed you off a letter which, I'm sure,
Will render things distinctly less obscure.
ALCESTE.
Well—let me have it!
CELIMENE.
     What *is* this all about?
ALCESTE.
God knows; but I have hopes of finding out.
How long am I to wait, you blitherer?
DUBOIS. *(After a protracted search for the letter.)*
I must have left it on your table, Sir.
ALCESTE.
I ought to...
CELIMENE.
    No, no, keep your self-control;
Go find out what's behind his rigmarole.
ALCESTE.
It seems that fate, no matter what I do,
Has sworn that I may not converse with you;
But, Madam, pray permit your faithful lover
To try once more before the day is over.

ACT V
SCENE ONE

ALCESTE, PHILINTE

ALCESTE.
No, it's too much. My mind's made up, I tell you.
PHILINTE.
Why should this blow, however hard, compel you...
ALCESTE.
No, no, don't waste your breath in argument;
Nothing you say will alter my intent;
This age is vile, and I've made up my mind
To have no further commerce with mankind.
Did not truth, honor, decency, and the laws
Oppose my enemy and approve my cause?
My claims were justified in all men's sight;
I put my trust in equity and right;
Yet, to my horror and the world's disgrace,
Justice is mocked, and I have lost my case!
A scoundrel whose dishonesty is notorious
Emerges from another lie victorious!
Honor and right condone his brazen fraud,
While rectitude and decency applaud!
Before his smirking face, the truth stands charmed,
And virtue conquered, and the law disarmed!
His crime is sanctioned by a court decree!
And not content with what he's done to me,
The dog now seeks to ruin me by stating
That I composed a book now circulating,

74

A book so wholly criminal and vicious
That even to speak its title is seditious!
Meanwhile Oronte, my rival, lends his credit
To the same libelous tale, and helps to spread it!
Oronte! a man of honor and of rank,
With whom I've been entirely fair and frank;
Who sought me out and forced me, willy-nilly,
To judge some verse I found extremely silly;
And who, because I properly refused
To flatter him, or see the truth abused,
Abets my enemy in a rotten slander!
There's the reward of honesty and candor!
The man will hate me to the end of time
For failing to commend his wretched rhyme!
And not this man alone, but all humanity
Do what they do from interest and vanity;
They prate of honor, truth, and righteousness,
But lie, betray, and swindle nonetheless.
Come then: man's villainy is too much to bear;
Let's leave this jungle and this jackal's lair.
Yes! treacherous and savage race of men,
You shall not look upon my face again.
PHILINTE.
Oh, don't rush into exile prematurely;
Things aren't as dreadful as you make them, surely.
It's rather obvious, since you're still at large,
That people don't believe your enemy's charge.
Indeed, his tale's so patently untrue
That it may do more harm to him than you.
ALCESTE.
Nothing could do that scoundrel any harm:
His frank corruption is his greatest charm,
And, far from hurting him, a further shame
Would only serve to magnify his name.
PHILINTE.
In any case, his bald prevarication

Has done no injury to your reputation,
And you may feel secure in that regard.
As for your lawsuit, it should not be hard
To have the case reopened, and contest
This judgement...
ALCESTE.

No, no, let the verdict rest.
Whatever cruel penalty it may bring,
I wouldn't have it changed for anything.
It shows the times' injustice with such clarity
That I shall pass it down to our posterity
As a great proof and signal demonstration
Of the black wickedness of this generation.
It may cost twenty thousand francs; but I
Shall pay their twenty thousand, and gain thereby
The right to storm and rage at human evil,
And send the race of mankind to the devil.
PHILINTE.
Listen to me...
ALCESTE.

Why? What can you possibly say?
Don't argue, Sir; your labor's thrown away.
Do you propose to offer lame excuses
For men's behavior and the times' abuses?
PHILINTE.
No, all you say I'll readily concede:
This is a low, dishonest age indeed;
Nothing but trickery prospers nowadays,
And people ought to mend their shabby ways.
Yes, man's a beastly creature; but must we then
Abandon the society of men?
Here in the world, each human frailty
Provides occasion for philosophy,
And that is virtue's noblest exercise;
If honesty shone forth from all men's eyes,
If every heart were frank and kind and just,

What could our virtues do but gather dust
(Since their employment is to help us bear
The villainies of men without despair)?
A heart well-armed with virtue can endure...
ALCESTE.
Sir, you're a matchless reasoner, to be sure;
Your words are fine and full of cogency;
But don't waste time and eloquence on me.
My reason bids me go, for my own good.
My tongue won't lie and flatter as it should;
God knows what frankness it might next commit,
And what I'd suffer on account of it.
Pray let me wait for Célimène's return
In peace and quiet. I shall shortly learn,
By her response to what I have in view,
Whether her love for me is feigned or true.
PHILINTE.
Till then, let's visit Eliante upstairs.
ALCESTE.
No, I am too weighed down with somber cares.
Go to her, do; and leave me with my gloom
Here in the darkened corner of this room.
PHILINTE.
Why, that's no sort of company, my friend;
I'll see if Eliante will not descend.

SCENE TWO

CELIMENE, ORONTE, ALCESTE

ORONTE.
Yes, Madam, if you wish me to remain
Your true and ardent lover, you must deign

To give me some more positive assurance.
All this suspense is quite beyond endurance.
If your heart shares the sweet desires of mine,
Show me as much by some convincing sign;
And here's the sign I urgently suggest:
That you no longer tolerate Alceste,
But sacrifice him to my love, and sever
All your relations with the man forever.
CELIMENE.
Why do you suddenly dislike him so?
You praised him to the skies not long ago.
ORONTE.
Madam, that's not the point. I'm here to find
Which way your tender feelings are inclined.
Choose, if you please, between Alceste and me,
And I shall stay or go accordingly.
ALCESTE. *(Emerging from the corner.)*
Yes, Madam, choose; this gentleman's demand
Is wholly just, and I support his stand.
I too am true and ardent; I too am here
To ask you that you make your feelings clear.
No more delays, now; no equivocation;
The time has come to make your declaration.
ORONTE.
Sir, I've no wish in any way to be
An obstacle to your felicity.
ALCESTE.
Sir, I've no wish to share her heart with you;
That may sound jealous, but at least it's true.
ORONTE.
If, weighing us, she leans in your direction...
ALCESTE.
If she regards you with the least affection...
ORONTE.
I swear I'll yield her to you there and then.

ALCESTE.
I swear I'll never see her face again.
ORONTE.
Now, Madam, tell us what we've come to hear.
ALCESTE.
Madam, speak openly and have no fear.
ORONTE.
Just say which one is to remain your lover.
ALCESTE.
Just name one name, and it will all be over.
ORONTE.
What! Is it possible that you're undecided?
ALCESTE.
What! Can your feelings possibly be divided?
CELIMENE.
Enough: this inquisition's gone too far:
How utterly unreasonable you are!
Not that I couldn't make the choice with ease;
My heart has no conflicting sympathies;
I know full well which one of you I favor,
And you'd not see me hesitate or waver.
But how can you expect me to reveal
So cruelly and bluntly what I feel?
I think it altogether too unpleasant
To choose between two men when both are present;
One's heart has means more subtle and more kind
Of letting its affections be divined,
Nor need one be uncharitably plain
To let a lover know he loves in vain.
ORONTE.
No, no, speak plainly; I for one can stand it.
I beg you to be frank.
ALCESTE.
                          And I demand it.
The simple truth is what I wish to know,
And there's no need for softening the blow.

You've made an art of pleasing everyone,
But now your days of coquetry are done:
You have no choice now, Madam, but to choose,
For I'll know what to think if you refuse;
I'll take your silence for a clear admission
That I'm entitled to my worst suspicion.
ORONTE.
I thank you for this ultimatum, Sir,
And I may say I heartily concur.
CELIMENE.
Really, this foolishness is very wearing:
Must you be so unjust and overbearing?
Haven't I told you why I must demur?
Ah, here's Eliante; I'll put the case to her.

SCENE THREE

ELIANTE, PHILINTE, CELIMENE, ORONTE, ALCESTE

CELIMENE.
Cousin, I'm being persecuted here
By these two persons, who, it would appear,
Will not be satisfied till I confess
Which one I love the more, and which the less,
And tell the latter to his face that he
Is henceforth banished from my company.
Tell me, has ever such a thing been done?
ELIANTE.
You'd best not turn to me; I'm not the one
To back you in a matter of this kind:
I'm all for those who frankly speak their mind.

ORONTE.
Madam, you'll search in vain for a defender.
ALCESTE.
You're beaten, Madam, and may as well surrender.
ORONTE.
Speak, speak, you must; and end this awful strain.
ALCESTE.
Or don't, and your position will be plain.
ORONTE.
A single word will close this painful scene.
ALCESTE.
But if you're silent, I'll know what you mean.

SCENE FOUR

ARSINOE, CELIMENE, ELIANTE, ALCESTE,
PHILINTE, ACASTE, CLITANDRE, ORONTE

ACASTE. *(To Célimène.)*
Madam, with all due deference, we two
Have come to pick a little bone with you.
CLITANDRE. *(To Oronte and Alceste.)*
I'm glad you're present, Sirs; as you'll soon learn,
Our business here is also your concern.
ARSINOE. *(To Célimène.)*
Madam, I visit you so soon again
Only because of these two gentlemen,
Who came to me indignant and aggrieved
About a crime too base to be believed.
Knowing your virtue, having such confidence in it,
I couldn't think you guilty for a minute,
In spite of all their telling evidence;
And, rising above our little difference,

I've hastened here in friendship's name to see
You clear yourself of this great calumny.
ACASTE.
Yes, Madam, let us see with what composure
You'll manage to respond to this disclosure.
You lately sent Clitandre this tender note.
CLITANDRE.
And this one, for Acaste, you also wrote.
ACASTE. *(To Oronte and Alceste.)*
You'll recognize this writing, Sirs, I think;
The lady is so free with pen and ink
That you must know it all too well, I fear.
But listen: This is something you should hear.

"How absurd you are to condemn my lightheartedness in
society, and to accuse me of being happiest in the company of
others. Nothing could be more unjust; and if you do not come to me
instantly and beg pardon for saying such a thing, I shall never
forgive you as long as I live. Our big bumbling friend the
Viscount..."

What a shame that he's not here.

"Our big bumbling friend the Viscount, whose name stands
first in your complaint, is hardly a man to my taste; and ever since
the day I watched him spend three-quarters of an hour spitting into
a well, so as to make circles in the water, I have been unable to
think highly of him. As for the little Marquess..."

In all modesty, gentleman that is I.

"As for the little Marquess, who sat squeezing my hand for such
a long while yesterday, I find him in all respects the most trifling
creature alive; and the only things of value about him are his cape
and his sword. As for the man with the green ribbons..."

(To Alceste.)
It's your turn now, Sir.

"As for the man with the green ribbons, he amuses me now and then with his bluntness and his bearish ill-humor; but there are many times indeed when I think him the greatest bore in the world. And as for the sonneteer..."

(To Oronte.)
Here's your helping.

"And as for the sonneteer, who has taken it into his head to be witty, and insists on being an author in the teeth of opinion, I simply cannot be bothered to listen to him, and his prose wearies me quite as much as his poetry. Be assured that I am not always so well-entertained as you suppose; that I long for your company, more than I dare to say, at all these entertainments to which people drag me; and that the presence of those one loves is the true and perfect seasoning to all one's pleasures."
CLITANDRE.
And now for me.

"Clitandre, whom you mention, and who so pesters me with his saccharine speeches, is the last man on earth for whom I could feel any affection. He is quite mad to suppose that I love him, and so are you, to doubt that you are loved. Do come to your senses; exchange your suppositions for his; and visit me as often as possible, to help me bear the annoyance of his unwelcome attentions."

It's a sweet character that these letters show,
And what to call it, Madam, you well know.
Enough. We're off to make the world acquainted
With this sublime self-portrait that you've painted.
ACASTE.
Madam, I'll make you no farewell oration;
No, you're not worthy of my indignation.

Far choicer hearts than yours, as you'll discover,
Would like this little Marquess for a lover.

SCENE FIVE

*CELIMENE, ELIANTE, ARSINOE, ALCESTE,
ORONTE, PHILINTE*

ORONTE.
So! After all those loving letters you wrote,
You turn on me like this, and cut my throat!
And your dissembling, faithless heart, I find,
Has pledged itself by turns to all mankind!
How blind I've been! But now I clearly see;
I thank you, Madam, for enlightening me.
My heart is mine once more, and I'm content;
The loss of it shall be your punishment.
(To Alceste.)
Sir, she is yours; I'll seek no more to stand
Between your wishes and this lady's hand.

SCENE SIX

*CELIMENE, ELIANTE, ARSINOE, ALCESTE,
PHILINTE*

ARSINOE. *(To Célimène.)*
Madam, I'm forced to speak. I'm far too stirred
To keep my counsel, after what I've heard.
I'm shocked and staggered by your want of morals.

It's not my way to mix in others' quarrels;
But really, when this fine and noble spirit,
This man of honor and surpassing merit,
Laid down the offering of his heart before you,
How *could* you...
ALCESTE.

                    Madam, permit me, I implore you,
To represent myself in this debate.
Don't bother, please, to be my advocate.
My heart, in any case, could not afford
To give your services their due reward;
And if I chose, for consolation's sake,
Some other lady, t'would not be you I'd take.
ARSINOE.
What makes you think you could, Sir? And how dare you
Imply that I've been trying to ensnare you?
If you can for a moment entertain
Such flattering fancies, you're extremely vain.
I'm not so interested as you suppose
In Célimène's discarded gigolos.
Get rid of that absurd illusion, do.
Women like me are not for such as you.
Stay with this creature, to whom you're so attached;
I've never seen two people better matched.

SCENE SEVEN

CELIMENE, ELIANTE, ALCESTE, PHILINTE

ALCESTE. *(To Célimène.)*
Well, I've been still throughout this exposé.
Till everyone but me has said his say.
Come, have I shown sufficient self-restraint?
And may I now...

85

CELIMENE.

Yes, make your just complaint.
Reproach me freely, call me what you will;
You've every right to say I've used you ill.
I've wronged you, I confess it; and in my shame
I'll make no effort to escape the blame.
The anger of those others I could despise;
My guilt toward you I sadly recognize.
Your wrath is wholly justified, I fear;
I know how culpable I must appear,
I know all things bespeak my treachery,
And that, in short, you've grounds for hating me.
Do so; I give you leave.
ALCESTE.

Ah, traitress—how,
How should I cease to love you, even now?
Though mind and will were passionately bent
On hating you, my heart would not consent.
(To Eliante and Philinte.)
Be witness to my madness, both of you;
See what infatuation drives one to;
But wait, my folly's only just begun,
And I shall prove to you before I'm done
How strange the human heart is, and how far
From rational we sorry creatures are.
(To Célimène.)
Woman, I'm willing to forget your shame,
And clothe your treacheries in a sweeter name;
I'll call them youthful errors, instead of crimes,
And lay the blame on these corrupting times.
My one condition is that you agree
To share my chosen fate, and fly with me
To that wild, trackless, solitary place
In which I shall forget the human race.
Only by such a course can you atone
For those atrocious letters; by that alone

Can you remove my present horror of you,
And make it possible for me to love you.
CELIMENE.
What! *I* renounce the world at my young age,
And die of boredom in some hermitage?
ALCESTE.
Ah, if you really loved me as you ought,
You wouldn't give the world a moment's thought;
Must you have me, and all the world beside?
CELIMENE.
Alas, at twenty one is terrified
Of solitude. I fear I lack the force
And depth of soul to take so stern a course.
But if my hand in marriage will content you,
Why, there's a plan which I might well consent to,
And...
ALCESTE.
   No, I detest you now. I could excuse
Everything else, but since you thus refuse
To love me wholly, as a wife should do,
And see the world in me, as I in you,
Go! I reject your hand, and disenthrall
My heart from your enchantments, once for all.

SCENE EIGHT

ELIANTE, ALCESTE, PHILINTE

ALCESTE. *(To Eliante.)*
Madam, your virtuous beauty has no peer;
Of all this world, you only are sincere;
I've long esteemed you highly, as you know;
Permit me ever to esteem you so,

And if I do not now request your hand,
Forgive me, Madam, and try to understand.
I feel unworthy of it; I sense that fate
Does not intend me for the married state,
That I should do you wrong by offering you
My shattered heart's unhappy residue,
And that in short...
ELIANTE.

               Your argument's well taken:
Nor need you fear that I shall feel forsaken.
Were I to offer him this hand of mine,
Your friend Philinte, I think, would not decline.
PHILINTE.
Ah, Madam, that's my heart's most cherished goal,
For which I'd gladly give my life and soul.
ALCESTE. *(To Eliante and Philinte.)*
May you be true to all you now profess,
And so deserve unending happiness.
Meanwhile, betrayed and wronged in everything,
I'll flee this bitter world where vice is king,
And seek some spot unpeopled and apart
Where I'll be free to have an honest heart.
PHILINTE.
Come, Madam, let's do everything we can
To change the mind of this unhappy man.